"He who lies to himself and listens to his own lies comes to a point where he cannot distinguish any truth either within himself or around him, and thus loses all respect for himself and for others. Lacking respect, he ceases to love, and without love, to occupy and distract himself, he gives in to passions and coarse pleasures, and in his vices reaches a state of bestiality, all because of his continuous lying to himself and to others."

(F. Dostoevsky, The Brothers Karamazov)

Summary

Introduction

Childhood and Teenage Years (1991 - 2011)

    Lost Innocence

    The House of Terror

    The Little Girl Decides to Speak Out

    The Separation and the Report

    The drawings begin to change

    The Trial and the Verdict

    The Price of Freedom

    Adolescence in the Balance

    A Slow Healing Process

Young years and other Traumas (2012 - 2024)

    Processing Trauma

    Another Sick Love

    A New Life

    Pandemic and Lockdown

    The day my mom died

    The Inheritance (or The Dissection)

    The Petition

    My 15 Minutes of Fame

The "Grieving" Widower

Nolite Te Bastardes Carborundorum

Acknowledgments

Introduction

When I think about my mother, the first memory that comes to mind is this song. I was standing on the bed, and she would lift me up with a huge smile, singing with a clear and harmonious voice: "I love you, you love me, we don't care about others... We are together, we love each other, we live." The happiest moments of my childhood—and I struggle to find them—were when she was there and when HE was not. Both sets of moments are very difficult to remember, for diametrically opposite reasons: for the first, because "there is no greater sorrow than to recall happy times in misery," as the famous Dante quote suggests; the others because they were only pain, misery, and suffering. HE is this entity that for me, my mother, and my sister, represents a kind of unnameable monster; WE will always call him HE and NEVER "father" or "dad"—or as my sister affectionately says, at most "the cockroach." So when you read the word HE, you will know who it corresponds to. Why go over all this? Some would tell me: no, you have to reset, stop thinking about the past. And others would add: exactly, this is just pure victimhood. Others still would say: yes, your story needs to be told. And why, I ask myself? Which voice should I listen to? I believe I must tell it, because too many people still think today that the term "violence against women" is almost expired like yogurt. Out of fashion, as if it were an outfit discarded by Ferragni (an Italian Top Influencer); something non-existent, exaggerated by "feminists who cry patriarchy"—yes, because many believe it is an insult to be a feminist—as I read in many male comments on the news of the many victims of femicide. My mother could have been one of them. This was and continues to be a reality; and it is terrible not only for women but also for children forced to live it. For many years, it was my reality, my mother's reality, my family's reality, and I cannot "reset and move on" without first telling it; it is a giant boulder I have always carried on my back and now I need to free myself from it and share the burden with others, to lighten it for those who have lived similar experiences to mine. I will narrate the facts from my point of view, reporting some excerpts from the verdict that took place in 2003 and other subsequent facts, some very recent, which do not concern the courts but highlight a marked tendency of the Italian Justice system to not protect victims of abuse and sexual harassment, even after their death.

Childhood and Teenage Years
(1991 - 2011)

Lost Innocence

I was a very creative, sweet, and "strange" child; I loved drawing, learning, imagining. Thinking back now, I miss that child so much and wonder how much of her remains in me, or if the events made her disappear, turning into an adult crushed by anger and pain.

I had many "peculiar" passions. One of them was the English language—for some inexplicable reason, given that no one in my family knew or spoke it. The only ones in the entire family tree, on both her and his side who went overseas, specifically to the USA, were my maternal great-grandparents; but they returned to Italy because they couldn't build the "American dream" and find fortune. I don't know if this has to do with my dream of learning English and living far away from my country, Italy.

I still remember when my mother and I went to a toy store one day. But I didn't want a toy: I asked my mother to buy me that beautiful illustrated blue English dictionary that immediately caught my eye in the book section. Its cover was shiny, and it somehow dazzled me: among all the store's sparkling toys, the light emanating from that dictionary was almost blinding to me.

"Are you sure you want this and not some toys?" my mother asked, surprised. And I said yes. Once home, I took one of my many notebooks where I used to draw, write, or jot down my thoughts and copied the illustrations and English words I found in the dictionary. When I learned something and drew it, I felt

"powerful"; knowledge was power, and I had just discovered it.
Another toy from my childhood—besides the countless Barbies—that I adored was a small keyboard of a strange yellowish color. I loved the sound of the notes it emitted and loved inventing new melodies, even though I wasn't particularly good at playing. Music, drawing, and English were my favorite hobbies at the age of six. This was the time when HE was gone.

As with any traumatic story worth its salt, unfortunately, the narration is never chronological: you remember many pieces of the puzzle and struggle to fit them together to make "order," but I am trying.

My mother was a petite woman, barely one meter and fifty-two centimeters tall—maybe a bit more, as she liked to convince herself to not feel too short. She had black eyes and raven hair, a smooth, soft face, and a heart-shaped mouth. Her eyes were so kind that as soon as you met them, you couldn't help but feel loved. Her body was always somewhat stocky—except when she was younger, and she was ashamed of it. My mother just wanted to be loved and to love. And she met someone who, unfortunately, was incapable of loving: HIM. My sister was born in 1987, and then I arrived in 1991. My mother later confided in me that she desperately prayed we would be girls; unlike HIM and his FAMILY, who wanted us to be boys. I'm happy I didn't satisfy his wish. I cannot know what happened in those four years before I was born, but I only have stories told to me by my sister, my mother, and other family members: I can only narrate what I experienced and saw; and that is what I will do.

My mother had no particular aspirations other than working hard to allow my sister and me to be well. But unfortunately, with a man like HIM, "well-being" could not be contemplated. And she realized it too late. They were opposites not only in terms of personality but also in appearance: she was so sweet, sensitive, and kind; HE was so coarse, arrogant, vulgar. She had harmonious facial features that inspired kindness. HE had stern, angular traits: a blade instead of a mouth, crooked teeth, a hooked nose, and cruel, expressionless eyes. Even their education levels were different: my mother was raised with an education emphasizing the importance of study; she had a diploma in accounting, while HE barely managed to get through middle school. Now that I think about it, during one of their countless fights, HE denigrated her by calling her "accountant." I know it was to humiliate her, from the tone he used, as if to say that despite her title, she was weak and stupid. The only thing they had in common was that their families came from Sicily: the maternal side from Catania and the paternal side from Palermo, both of their families had emigrated to Milan. Other things I remember about him: he smoked like a chimney, smelled bad, loved alcohol—probably drugs and prostitutes too—always went out in the evening and often returned late at night. Doing what, I don't know, but every time he came back, the terror infested all the serenity that my mother transmitted.

Our house was really small, less than fifty square meters for four people. A house that was paid for almost entirely by my mother and her job as an employee since HE did odd jobs, but most of the time, he was unemployed. An entrance with a long, narrow corridor, leading to the left to the small kitchen and balcony; a small bathroom and finally the bedroom, which was quite large, with a double bed and a single bed for my sister, from which another bed was pulled out for me. I'm not clear on this point, but perhaps that bed broke at some point—mine, probably because I jumped on it, and this was the result—so we ended up sleeping together in the same big bed, my mother, my sister, and I.

The House of Terror

Sometimes, I recall that awful feeling when he would come home at night and get into bed, perhaps next to me. Nothing would happen, but the thought of him being so close terrified and disgusted me. In my head, I would repeat, "Don't move, you're asleep, he won't do anything to you." HE loved hitting my mother when he was home; I never knew the reason and I believe, I never will. Ignorance, lack of empathy, mental disorders, a loveless childhood, alcohol, and drug abuse? Perhaps all of these together. For years, as a teenager and an adult, I studied, even to understand all this. Still today, I don't know if I've come to a conclusion. In those moments, when he "transformed" into a serial abuser, anger took hold of me in my little child's body: I wanted to stop him and hit him, or rather, I wanted him to die. Yes, that was what he made me feel, at an age when death should be a thought for grown-ups and certainly not directed at someone who should be a "parent". The kitchen was HIS favorite place to hit my mother. Here I remember a scene that is still imprinted in my mind as if it were a freshly taken photograph. And I remember many others, there, in different places and with HIM as the protagonist: indelible photos that often accompanied me in nightmares and my adult life. I don't remember how old I was, but it must have been before they separated (in 1998): I think I was about four or five years old. In this terrible snapshot, HE got angry one day for some trivial reason. He forcefully threw my mother to the other end of the wall, and I heard an unpleasant sound, like a stone hitting a hard surface; she landed on the couch and started crying. A halo of urine began spreading on the couch, creating a dark stain. Yes, that's what HE could trigger: such fear that one would wet oneself. My mother was hunched over as if to protect herself and cried from fear and shame. Perhaps also from anger, because she felt helpless, fragile, destroyed. At that point, HE mocked her for wetting herself. I don't remember the exact words, but I remember very well my growing disgust at hearing them. He said something like, "Look how ridiculous you are" or something similar. I, who had watched the scene in disbelief and horror, hugged my mother and then threw myself forcefully at HIM, shouting: "Why do you do this to her, why? You're bad!" I tried to punch him. HE did not respond and did not react. I was such a small child that my father seemed like a giant to me—in reality, only as an adult did I realize he was below average male height. I must have seemed to him like a little ant trying to fend off a queen bee; he didn't even bother to stop me, as if my punches were as threatening as caresses. In the kitchen, I remember another photo of us eating around the table: we usually moved the part that adhered to the wall to let HIM sit, because as he always said: "the man is the head, so he must be at the head of the table." In that snapshot, we had ordered pizza, and my sister and I were happy—I assume my mother was too, as she didn't have to cook, given that she worked a lot and was always tired, unlike HIM. I remember the TV volume was quite high, and my father was absorbed in watching it. Then my sister and I finished eating, leaving the pizza crusts on the plate because we didn't like them. One of us asked my mother, "Can we go play now?" My mother didn't have time to answer. Suddenly, the TV volume went down. My father looked at us intently, then observed our plates with the crusts left. "You haven't finished until the plate is clean. If you don't eat everything, I'll get the belt from the drawer, and you'll see..." He had already threatened to beat us with that belt several times. My sister and I quickly sat down, and the TV volume resumed as before. We finished those damn crusts, then went to play. I remember that when HE wasn't home, we could breathe a sigh of relief, and life was like a huge weight lifted off. But when he returned, I felt like I had to hold my breath, always be alert to his slightest move, every outburst, or word he said. We couldn't do anything to prevent it: he would often lash out for trivial reasons; and he shouted, A LOT. That's why as an adult I developed post-traumatic stress disorder—and not just that, unfortunately—in fact, whenever someone makes a sudden move, I get a sort of panic attack. This also happens when someone SHOUTS: for me, it's a sign of danger, an alarm, as if something bad is about to happen. Another aspect that always troubled me was "fights": for years, I associated the word fight with HATE and VIOLENCE because that's what I had always seen and experienced. So much so that when I happened to fight with my mother, I was terrified to the point of asking her, "Now that we fought, do you hate me? Do you not love me anymore?"

My mother, at these questions, would look at me with sweetness and also with a veil of sadness, aware that what I had lived had somehow altered my sense of "normality." "No, you don't have to worry that I don't love you, it's impossible for me not to love you. We can fight, that doesn't mean we hate each other," she would reply, hugging me. I then felt relieved at those moments; yet I didn't understand why the fights with my mother were so different from those between her and HIM.

In other scenes, I remember HE would tell me "I love you" and even: "I love you." One day, as an adult, I told a friend about this, who is no longer my friend. She said to me: "You're lucky, my father never said that to me. If he said that, then he can't be that bad." Dear Biancaurora, I hope you read this book one day, so maybe you'll apologize for your words. Going back to his "I love you," at those moments, I thought that if this was his way of loving, there must be something wrong—not just with HIM—but with the words too. Because children tend to generalize, they can't abstract like: "It's his words I should distrust, not all"; and especially not the meaning of the word "love." So, I began to distrust words and become a silent child, especially in his presence. At those moments, when asked "why is he so bad," I answered myself: because he's ignorant. I was barely five or six years old and understood that a man so bad must be so because he was ignorant; not just because he hadn't studied, but also because he "ignored" the fact that he was hurting us. I decided I would become a studious child, I would read, try to understand why things were the way they were. As a child, I wanted only one thing, maybe two. NOT TO BE LIKE HIM and for HIM TO DISAPPEAR FOREVER.

The Little Girl Decides to Speak Out

My wish never came true: I managed not to become like him, but I couldn't make him disappear forever. Despite praying every night for his death, my prayers went unanswered. That's why, in the following years, I lost the faith instilled by catechism. One day, I told my mother that I didn't believe in an entity that couldn't be seen. Moreover, I couldn't believe in an entity that caused so much pain, not just to me, but to so many people.

So I decided—unconsciously—that to make HIM disappear, I had to speak out. Finally, I understood that words had power, and I couldn't let that power fade within me because of HIS words. I was in kindergarten when I decided to tell a classmate what was going on in the house. I told everything: of my father's favorite hobby, that is to beat my mother, but also of other hobbies that reserved for us daughters. He really liked touching us right there in that organ that separates us from males. I remember a very unpleasant photograph about it, the ugliest in my horror album called HIM: we were in the car. He had stopped at a remote location, near his work place at the time. I was sitting in front of him, next to him, and I was worried that he stopped. After a few minutes of silence, he looked at me and with his hand went to feel me right there, for a time that seemed endless. It was like everything was moving in slow motion: I just wanted to scream, to run away, but I was trapped, like a little fly in a spider's web - that's why I've always been arachnophobic. When she finished touching me, I was so horrified and stiff with humiliation and helplessness that I was in shock. It happened other times, but I don't remember the details. The things I didn't remember, I read years later in the trial papers. That day I told my kindergarten classmate that my dad would touch me "here", pointing to a doll where the vagina should be. The teacher, who was nearby, heard everything and asked me questions I don't remember now. I just know she was shocked, eyes wide open. He called my mother right away. He told her what I had said and uttered this sentence, which I will never forget: "Madam, you must immediately ask for separation and report him to the police. There is a risk that they will take away her daughters". I think my mother, once she heard this, felt the biggest nightmare of her life: she endured everything, the beatings, the threats, the humiliations. But this NO, it was really too much. Because if I'm sure of one thing in life, it's that she would throw herself into the fire to save us.

Judgment of the Court of First Instance, 2003:

I. S. was an educator of Desirèe Gullo, from September 1996 to June 1997, for an entire school year. The child seemed calm, but at certain times she had a crying crisis, for example towards the beginning of the year 1997; in these situations she showed symptoms of depression, and she isolated herself a little from the other children, but did not reveal why she cried. Then the mother told them that she and her husband had separated, and that her husband had gone to live in another house. In October 1996, Desirèe told her that her mother and father had argued, and her father had pushed her mother against the wall or against the window, because her father had kissed her little sister on the mouth, and her mother was angry. The child was still very closed, even if she seemed more mature than her age; she spoke little of herself and much more willingly of her sister, to whom she was very fond. In the spring of 1997 the little girl, while in class she was playing with the buildings, almost screaming, said "Dad always touches me, he touches me here and I don't want to", but it was not addressed to anyone in particular. Having given no weight to the first episode, they were worried by the second they tried to deepen, he told her to draw what a child did with his father; at first he cried, then in the drawings he represented the genital area, even if covered by clothes, it was always colored red; Then she talked about games on the couch, but the phrase she used to say was that her father touched her potato chip. Another time the little girl said Dad always gives me kisses and says "I love you". He also said: "Dad came to get me and in the car he touched me".

At this point I would also like to add the parts that concern my sister; albeit partially because I respect her decision not to want to reopen this "pandora's box". I will mention only a part of the sentence, for completeness of information, concerning the teachers of my sister who at that time attended elementary school.

[...]they had been informed by the principal that their little sister, attending the

kindergarten in via Rimini, had reported that the father had taken on special attitudes towards him; so they had been told to pay attention to any possible "Particular signs" in the other girl [...] the little girl told her the same day that her father touched her. The little girl had cried in front of her colleague [...] had no more crisis, but still cried; he told her "let me play, don't let me think"; and he added only that he did not want to go with Dad because he touched her, and pointed at her breasts and intimate parts, saying that it also hurt her (it was the period of development). The girl was very smart, an excellent student, very good from the point of view of teaching, open and spontaneous.
He told her that even with her little sister the father did so, but being the younger sister was less annoying, because he did not realize.

On this last point I would object, even if I was little, I realized, unfortunately. Maybe she meant that at that age I had less awareness of what was happening; but these facts have made me acquire a consciousness that for my age was almost that of an adult.

She said that his mother knew and intervened on his behalf, but was afraid of his father: in these cases the father took it out on his mother. Mom would almost always come to the interviews, they only saw the father sometimes, when he picked up the child at the exit.

The Separation and the Report

My mother obtained the separation on February 25, 1998. I didn't remember this date, but I discovered it by requesting the document from her lawyer at the time, once I became an adult. I have some memories of this lawyer, mainly from my mother's accounts. She said she was a cold woman, emotionless, and my mother often left her office crying; once the lawyer met HIM and said these exact words: "I met your husband and he doesn't seem like a bad person."

From that moment on, I began to distrust lawyers, and I believe my mother did too. In the separation agreement, which I only noticed now, there are some chilling details. It reads in the consensual separation: "The spouses will live separately with the obligation of mutual respect." From HIS SIDE, there was never any RESPECT. I will explain why later. And again: "The mother will provide for the maintenance of the daughters because the father, currently unemployed, is unable to contribute." This is truly appalling, considering the many separated men who currently complain about having to pay alimony to their wives. Finally, the icing on the cake: "The registration fees will be borne in full by the wife." The law "supported" all this, without even remotely protecting my mother; but we are only at the beginning of the story.

And so, HE finally left the house. I believe my mother had to have him removed by the police, otherwise I doubt he would have left voluntarily. Following the separation, there was a report for domestic violence and sexual harassment of minors, namely us two, his daughters.

I remember when my mother went to the barracks to report him: she took me with her because I was still too young to be left alone at home. Of that barracks, I remember more of the outside environment than the inside: I have a faded image of a sort of room with tables and ivy expanding on trellises. I absolutely don't remember what happened inside the barracks. I remember the "before," when we were still at home and my mother told me we had to go there.

"I have to do it," she said to me, "there is a risk they will take you away from me." Her tears broke my heart in two halves: one for absolute love towards her, the other became a stone forged from hatred towards HIM. I replied candidly, as only children can do: "Mom, how is it possible that they take you away from us? Everyone will realize what a good mother you are, you don't have to be afraid of this." After these words, my mother burst into tears even more, but this time it seemed more like a cry of relief. I also felt like crying, but I decided I had to be strong for her. So, I took one of my drawings to wipe away her tears. The tears faded the drawing, ruining it.

"I'm sorry I ruined your drawing."

"Don't worry, Mom, I'll make another one."

And so, we left home and went to report my father.

One day, the police came to our house and told us they were looking for him, but they couldn't find him. They probably had to notify him of the report. They asked my mother what car he had. She didn't know, but I did because that was the car where I experienced my biggest trauma.

"It's a small white car," I replied.

I think it was a Fiat Punto.

Life without HIM began in our house, but not in our lives. I remember that as soon as my mother reported him and he left home, I felt relieved of a huge burden. But another phase began. The court rightly gave sole custody to my mother, but allowed HIM to see us sporadically, in his new home, with his new woman. How is it possible for a violent and molesting man to continue seeing his daughters? A lawyer or a jurist would immediately have a ready answer: the presumption of innocence prevails until there is a final conviction. But this is not "ethically" right.

So, we had to endure these painful "journeys" to his new woman's house, named Rosa. My mother told me, once I became an adult, that Rosa was probably a prostitute. I remember she had two sons. During those trips, we found ourselves in this new "family," and I didn't want to be there. One day, I was on the couch watching TV and my father was next to me. He said something like, "I love you."

"I don't," I replied sharply.

"Why?" HE asked.

"Because you are a bad man."

Children's truth is candid, direct, like a boxer's right hook. But I don't think HE was hurt by it. I don't remember his response, but he took it lightly, as if it were nonsense said by a little girl. He wasn't smart enough to understand that he had stolen my childhood and that I was now a little adult, mature beyond my years. Fortunately, I inherited intelligence from my mother.

My memories of Rosa are neither positive nor particularly unpleasant. I didn't like her character; I kept thinking, "She is so different from my mother, so unkind and ignorant, like HIM." This may seem trivial, but it gave me an unpleasant feeling, as if she resented having to "take care of me." I found some information about Rosa even in the First Instance Judgment of 2003.

The defendant is guilty of the crime referred to in art. 572 of the Italian Penal

Code for mistreating his cohabitant C. Rosa, causing her continuous beatings, even during a state of pregnancy resulting in abortion, physical and moral harassment, also connected with the abuse of alcoholic substances, extremely harsh living conditions.

Only my sister could testify to the worst memory that happened in that house because I wasn't there. I know one day my father beat her in Rosa's house. She said nothing; HE also beat her. So they took my sister home. My mother, seeing her with a black eye, was shocked and got so mad that she forced the court to prevent him from visiting. At that point, the process for the report accelerated, and my father was prevented from approaching our home. HE, of course, did not respect this provision. He began to threaten us with death by phone, intercom, and letter. The intercom always rang, every night at two, three, four in the morning. We were forced to unplug the intercom and let it hang down to avoid hearing the noise.

One day, my mother went downstairs to make him stop. I must say that I don't remember this fact, but my sister told me about it as an adult. She told me that after our mother decided to confront him, we were both in total panic: we feared that our mother would not return and that he would kill her. Because that's what he kept shouting on the intercom, and once I heard it: "If you don't let me in, I'll break down the door and kill you, ALL of you."

But fortunately, our mother came back.

The drawings begin to change

Yes, I was a very good child at drawing. But the day after that incident, when I went to school, I remember that at one point we had to color a frame for our Italian notebook. I don't remember which grade I was in, but I presume it was between first and second grade. I colored it very poorly and my teacher seemed troubled by it. Once it was time for recess, Michela - the Italian teacher - called me and asked me to sit on her lap.

"Desy, why did you color so poorly? You always color so well, did something happen?"

I was amazed at how my teacher could understand my state of unease from a simple drawing. I lowered my gaze, staring at my feet, and whispered what was happening. "Last night my father threatened us with death at the intercom, I was scared." The teacher hugged me gently, stroking my hair, and said in a sweet voice, "I'm so sorry, sweetheart. You were very brave to tell me."

I remember many other situations where my teacher showed sensitivity and respect for my situation, not just mine. For example, when the Father's Day celebration came around and we were making crafts or greeting cards for "fathers." In my class, there were two of us who didn't have a father, for different reasons: me, for everything I've recounted so far, and then there was my best friend Angela, who had lost her father when she was little. In those moments, I remember the teacher telling us to make the same craft but for our mothers; the same thing happened when we were assigned the topic about fathers. Our teacher told us to write the essay about our mother, being the only parent we had who also played the role of "father" for us. I confided in my friend Angela about part of what I was going through, and I remember telling her this once: "If only we could switch, I wish my father were dead instead of yours." I don't remember how she reacted, but she was certainly very struck by my words.

These school events were just part of my daily life. Meanwhile, social workers often came to our house to check that my mother was "fit" in her role; and indeed, she was declared so. This was followed by visits from psychologists, which were numerous; I remember two in particular. In one of these visits, we went to a center (in Italy is called the Neutral Space, for minors who have been abused) that was bordered by a beautiful garden. When we entered, they administered - separately - the Rorschach test to us. I didn't know what it was about, nor have I ever known the results of that test, not even as an adult. I just know that I was asked to analyze those images and understand what I saw in them; it seemed very funny and entertaining to me, actually. I only remember that in one of those images I saw a bra - who knows what that was supposed to mean. In another visit, only my mother and I went: the place was different and I remember my mother accompanied me to a psychologist, who then asked her to wait outside. He asked me to make a drawing representing my family: I remember I liked it a lot, since I loved to draw. The drawing I made, I don't know why, was set outdoors, in a garden: I remember using the color green for the grass, the plants, and then a pond in the center. It was a very lively and happy drawing; perhaps it was my attempt to respond to the trauma, as if I was looking for an oasis of happiness in which to find refuge from the storm I had around me.

The days, despite everything, passed quite calmly. I was happy to go to school and that part of my life was the only happy parenthesis of that period. But then from time to time, we would hear news about HIM. And that apparent calm would suddenly vanish. Every time my mother went to pick up the mail, about every week, we found strange postcards sent by HIM. I use the term "strange" especially for the different images on them; I only remember one in particular. It was the background of a farm, with cows in the foreground; I think there was a rather large cow and the others were smaller. The oddity, besides the choice of the image, was that next to the first cow there was an arrow - written by him in pen - with the following words, "Mom"; then next to the other cows he put my name and that of my sister. The content of these postcards I could define as "bipolar" because, in them, the main theme was that he would kill us all, but then he often added that he missed us and wrote, addressed to me and I think also to my sister: "I love you."

These postcards, in addition to the continuous death threats at the intercom, disrupted our family life that we were trying to rebuild. I think it was HIS attempt to say to us: "You haven't gotten rid of me and you never will; I still control your life." These postcards were subsequently used in the trial, because they clearly indicated his death threats against us. When I contacted the lawyer, many years later, to retrieve these postcards as "evidence" for another more recent matter, she told me they were no longer there; he blamed the archivist of the time. Even now I wonder how they could have disappeared.

One day, still in the kitchen - which for some strange reason seemed to be the stage of some dark tragedy - I stood on the threshold watching my mother. In the same spot where, years before, I had incredulously watched HIM throw my mother against the wall. She was now taking something from the kitchen cabinet: it was one of those white plastic packages, perhaps for cleaning the floor. I watched as she opened the bottle and brought it to her throat, while a desolate cry played in the background of her gesture.

"Mom, what are you doing? Have you gone mad?" I yelled at her, shocked by what I had seen. She abruptly lowered the arm with which she held the bottle and closed it. Her gaze was alarmed with eyes wide open with terror: I don't know if more frightened by the gesture she was about to make or by the fact that I had seen her doing it.

"I'm sorry, you know I would never have done it!" she said to me, desperate, sobbing.

I went to hug her and we cried together.

"I'm just very desperate, I can't take it anymore," she said.

"I know, but we're going to survive all of this, you'll see," I said to comfort her. But I was truly traumatized by that scene and for years I wondered what would have happened if I hadn't been there to witness it. My mother later told me that my words, "we're going to survive all of this" gave her the strength to move forward.

The Trial and the Verdict

It is well known that the "Justice" process in Italy is lengthy. From the moment of reporting to the trial, two or three years passed; from the moment of reporting to the first-instance sentence, five years elapsed. During that time, evidence, testimonies, and reports from social workers, educators, psychologists, and teachers had to be gathered.

Once all this was collected, my sister and I were summoned to the Milan court, in what is called the "protected courtroom," dedicated to minors who, due to their age and involvement in such delicate dynamics, cannot testify in a regular courtroom. We were interviewed separately; when I was called in, I sat in a chair that, in my memories, had an ancient, almost baroque style. It was a rectangular room, with a predominant gray color, at least that's how I remember it.

In front of me, besides the microphone recording my deposition - which would later be heard in court along with my sister's - I noticed two or three people. I mainly remember a fairly young woman who asked me terrible questions that I struggled to answer.

"How did he touch you? Did he grip? Rub against you? Did it hurt? With an open hand? With a closed hand? How did he hold his fingers? Did he move them like this, can you show me?" I answered with difficulty, crying. To help me answer, the woman mimicked everything she was asking, and this detail made the situation even more unbearable. I felt humiliated, both by what had happened and by those questions. I understood why they were asking these questions, but I just wanted to shout for them to stop, that there was no need to ask me all those stupid questions: he simply touched me, and it wasn't normal for a "dad" doing it! I felt like I was the one guilty, and I kept asking myself why they didn't go to him and ask this - but I suppose they did.

Basically, they wanted to know if this man was having a sexual pleasure by doing this to his daughters. Well I think it is common, for every narcissist like him, feeling pleasure: by humiliating, beating or molesting us. That was his language, throughout he expressed his insane and distorted "love". Actually from the deposition act that I have - obtained later, as an adult - I've understood lots of things that I couldn't, back then but could only sense.

Here there is an excerpt from the verdict and part of the deposition I gave, transcribed in the verdict.

The object of the complaint, which the educators communicated to the mother, consisted in the fact that Desirèe said that "the father touched her"; Dr. R entered with the lady even more on the merits, explaining to the woman that it was sexual touching, and that the child no longer wished to be alone with her father, because the man took advantage of it to make her undress and perform improper acts. Desirée was heard, with the assistance of auxiliary psychologist, in a room adjacent to the courtroom, in audiovisual connection with the courtroom itself. The father beat his mother and sister, and touched her and her sister, in the sense that he touched their private parts. This happened when she was six or seven years old; the facts also happened at home, but rarely, and more often in the car. For example, once he was in the car with him, in the presence of his sister, the father drove and touched her. The touches happened when they were dressed. He repeated that the father extended his hand, and touched it from above his clothes, with all his hand. She doesn't remember if her hand stayed still or not. Sometimes Simona was also present, sometimes she and her father were alone. Nothing happened other than that. When it happened in the house, the place was always the kitchen, near the sofa, but he does not remember well what was happening in the house, he remembers well only the car. She got along with Dad, but not when he did those things. Currently her father calls her, but she doesn't want to be called, she doesn't want to hear it. There were no occasions when the father played with her and touched her elsewhere, even for fun. She doesn't remember if her father pinched her: "pinch no, touch yes". She told him that it bothered her, she told him to stop. The mother understood what was happening, and defended them, but the father beat her. The father never asked her to do anything about him.

For HIM those gestures were of "affection": it was normal - his words - because he had been used so. Then he added: "If I had boys I would have done the same, I would have touched them kindly saying, Daddy's pretty dick." Of course, it was all normal. Except that it was absolutely not. I also read a report by the court psychiatrist, who analyzed HIM and his deviated mind. And it detected the following characteristics.

Cultivated arrogance, intolerance of limits, propensity to satisfy impulses, impulsiveness, pronounced tendency to control others, which in reality seem to cover deep insecurity, significant difficulties in interpersonal relationships, and instances of depression.

In addition, the judgment also includes the following about HIM:

"[...] Stand out the spontaneous statements made by the defendant, who, with his own grossly misleading interpretation of the behaviors towards his daughters, showed an absolute lack of remorse. For completeness of argumentation, it should be mentioned that, in light of their inherent and completely unequivocal nature of sexual intrusiveness and the explicit and repeated request to desist made by the very young daughters, Gullo's actions must be considered not only objectively criminal but also with an evident malicious connotation.

In the first-instance judgment of 2003, HE was sentenced to 3 years and 6 months in prison, declared to have forfeited parental authority and succession rights. Moreover, he was required to compensate the victims, namely my mother, myself, and my sister. The court determined the compensation as follows: twelve thousand euros for me, twelve thousand euros for my sister, plus reimbursement of expenses amounting to four thousand euros; for my mother, the compensation was eight thousand euros plus procedural costs of four thousand euros. WE NEVER RECEIVED THE COMPENSATION, the court did nothing to verify that this compensation was paid, nor did my mother's lawyer do anything to request this payment. In all this, he did not even tell her that she should have asked for a divorce, to prevent him from having rights over her property in the future - since the Italian law does not provide for disqualification from succession in cases of spouse abuse, but only in cases of spousal homicide.

We will address this part later.

The Price of Freedom

Our family dynamic had changed, and despite the negative consequences, once at home, we felt immense relief in finally being "free" from his presence. However, I realized during elementary school that freedom came with a very high price. My mother had to go into debt to pay for her lawyer, and we plunged into a situation of economic precariousness, to the point where we were forced to ask the neighborhood shops for "credit." It used to be like this: the shopkeepers knew my mother and allowed us to mark down what we bought and pay later.

This situation of deep economic distress continued somewhat steadily until middle and high school, despite occasional periods when my mother obtained loans and we managed to breathe for a while. But then that money had to be repaid, and it felt like we had navigated through a stormy sea only to have lightning strike our lifeboat, tossing us back into the open sea. My life has been like this, a continuous struggle against towering waves in an endless storm of wind, without the tools to swim and stay afloat, never managing to reach a calm harbor: a life in constant breath-holding, one could say.

The only "happy oasis" where we could catch our breath was my maternal grandparents' house in Villa Verucchio, near Rimini. We spent our summers there, and my grandparents were very important figures for us. They had an immense garden where my sister and I could experience the carefreeness that had been taken away from us: we felt liberated, as if we were butterflies whose wings had been clipped and could finally take flight. But then, when it was time to go home, we returned to our "imprisonment": at the mercy of events, trapped in a black hole from which we couldn't see the light. In those periods when we literally had "not a penny," I remember that my mother, being employed in the offices of a large supermarket chain, almost always brought home food that her company left for employees. My mother told us how lucky she was to work in the "meat" department. When she was later transferred to the "gardening and miscellaneous goods" department, things changed, and unfortunately, we could no longer enjoy all that free food. I still remember my mother's famous phrases when she had to deny us toys or other expenses: "we can't spend anything because we're broke," or "if we keep this up, we'll end up flat broke." Despite the dramatic situation, looking back now, these phrases make me smile. My mother sometimes had the ability to turn drama into a kind of tragicomic show: she had a subtle irony and often tried to make us laugh with funny stories. For example, before bed, she would tell us crazy stories about a certain Pierino and his misadventures (usually involving Pierino making a fool of himself), and we would laugh uproariously.

I also remember that she often took us to the cinema and on various outings: one that I particularly remember is to Parco di

Porta Venenzia in Milan. There was a carriage with horses, and she took us for a ride there: that moment was truly beautiful and surreal, I felt happy and important; I had never felt like that in daily life. Around seven or eight years old, I began to develop a very particular hobby: since we were now on the brink of poverty, I started putting myself in the shoes of the many beggars I saw on the street. Along Corso San Gottardo in Milan, there was once "Upim," a clothing store, and "Sma," a supermarket. In front of the entrance, there was always the same beggar with his dog, and I often passed by there to shop with my mother. I tried to convince her to give him some coins, but she would tell me that we couldn't afford it. Sometimes, I managed to make her relent. So, I would go to give him the coin and I would feel good. But I didn't stop there: I often left coins around on sidewalks or benches; coins that I had saved from gifts given by my aunts or grandparents. "Why do you leave coins like that on the street?" my mother asked me, surprised. "Because that way, someone who is poor can find them and be happier." I don't remember exactly how my mother reacted at that point; I just remember her warm smile that overwhelmed me, as if she couldn't believe that from this hell, I had remained somehow "untouched" in my goodness.

Throughout this period, my father contributed nothing, and even the act of separation allowed this, as he was considered "penniless." So my mother, with her small salary as an employee, was alone in supporting her family. To do this, she had to take out numerous loans, which were used to pay lawyers and accumulating expenses, resulting in debts. In addition to work, debts, and her daughters, she also had to follow the legal proceedings, always fearing retaliation from the other side, always anxious about not being able to manage everything. I don't know how she managed not to go crazy.

I remember once she came to pick me up from school and had a sort of fainting spell, as if she lacked the strength to walk. Indeed, she clung to the fence that bordered the elementary school, and I was upset by all of this. "Mom, what's wrong?" I asked, worried. "Nothing, I'm just tired," I think she replied. She always said she was so tired, and only as an adult did I truly understand the meaning of her fatigue. A woman who, like David, had to fight against Goliath, HIM, the courts, JUSTICE; who worked from eight in the morning and came home at seven in the evening, who had to take care of two children alone, how could she not be tired? When I got older and reminded her of this episode, she told me that at that time she suffered from panic attacks, and that's where one manifested.

One day we were walking the same street, when she said a phrase that struck me to the heart, filling it with unexpected happiness. "I've thought about it and yes, we can get a cat," she said, looking at me smiling, as if she expected my incredulous reaction, which indeed happened. My sister and I at the time insisted on having a cat, but my mother didn't agree: not because she didn't love animals, but because, having so many worries to think about, it seemed like an additional burden to take care of. But for some reason, which she confided in me later, she changed her mind. I think I shouted with joy and hugged her in that moment; I couldn't believe it! So coming home, I announced the news to my sister, who probably reacted in the same way. My mother took a newspaper where they put animal announcements and started reading some, until she read one that caught her and our attention: "giving away a red cat and a white and brown cat, they are sisters."

To our question, "can we take both of them," my mother obviously replied with a firm no, "one is enough, the house is too small." She contacted the person from the ad and the next day we went to the meeting: the man had brought both cats in the car, in their carriers. My sister and I couldn't decide which one to take of the two, it seemed such a bad thing to separate them...But a choice had to be made. For some inexplicable reason, my mother asked me to choose. And I chose the red kitten, whom we called "Milù." When we brought her home, I remember she hid all the time under a chest that we had in the hallway. My sister and I were worried that she would never want to come out, but my mother reassured us, telling us that she probably needed time to get used to it, being a new home for her. In fact, the next day she came out and started exploring the surrounding environment: my sister and I played with her every time we came home and for us it was an incredible joy to have a cat. Our mood improved decisively and so did that of our mother. Of course, I admit that being small we did some mischief to our Milù, who promptly scratched us. But, especially after a few years, she began to be more and more affectionate towards us: she would lie down with us in bed and relax us by being next to us.

My mother later confided to me why she had changed her mind.

"During that time you were very sad. I felt guilty, I didn't know what to do to make you feel better. So, since you had insisted for a long time, I decided to do it, for you."

Adolescence in the Balance

I have nothing to add about my middle school years, except that it was a disaster on all fronts, except for academics. And things worsened in high school. I remember this phase as a very dark period, full of loneliness, hopelessness, and sadness, like a sky without stars. In Italy our High School system is quite different from the European or American ones: the high schools are divided by argument like Classical, Scientific, Artistic, Social Sciences and then there are the "professional schools" for those that are not really into "studying" but they prefer learning a job quickly - without attending University - and to be a worker soon.

I attended an Artistic High School, and I was a bright student. But in the third year, I refused to go to school: I was ashamed to leave the house, ashamed of myself and my appearance; this was greatly influenced by the bullying I had endured for so many years.

So, I decided to change schools and spent a year at home studying, as I had to take an entrance exam for the next school, the High School of Social Sciences. During that year at home, the only escapes from pain for me were reading, drawing, and music. The few friends I had disappeared. And I felt completely alone.

I often argued with my mother because I didn't know who to blame for how my life was going: downhill, in free fall, amidst physical and hormonal transformation and a background resembling a Greek tragedy. I often asked her why, why she had married him, why she had made me so unhappy. My tone was often hostile, typically adolescent; yet I am ashamed of all this now as I look back. But back then, I couldn't understand: it was reading that saved me. I began to have a strong desire to read everything I had at home; the books were few, mostly books my sister had to buy because they were assigned as Italian readings. So I started with a book I found right on the shelf above my sister's computer, it was called "The Catcher in the Rye" and it immediately attracted me. Then I started going to the Libraccio - a book shop - because there I could buy many used books at a low cost. I became very passionate about Dostoevsky and in particular about "Crime and Punishment" for various reasons: for the theme of social disparities, for the fact that it tells of a poor person who commits a desperate act because he doesn't know how to survive anymore; because it makes it clear that Justice tends to beat the poor and instead lay out a red carpet for the rich, to those who kill during wars. I felt just like them: like the young Holden who couldn't find his own way, in a world that seemed to be a one-way street; like Raskolnikov, who tried to emancipate himself from his condition of poverty and discomfort, but who was trapped in a path that society had already chosen for him.

The book that most opened my eyes to what I had experienced was "Women Who Love Too Much" by Robin Norwood. I unexpectedly found it in my mother's bedside table, in her room. I didn't know she had read it and I was curious. This book allowed me to understand why certain women - like my mother - tend to be attracted to narcissistic, manipulative, and sometimes violent men and that is due to lack of self-esteem, above all. And also because many of these women, unfortunately, have had a family history of violence, perpetrated by the father figure against the mother figure. So, unconsciously, as adults they tend to relive the same trauma, seeking a male figure similar to the paternal one, for two particular reasons: to try to "face" the unresolved trauma and because human beings are inclined to seek people who are similar to their own family life. It had been the same for my mother.

At that moment, when I realized all this, I empathized with my mother in a way that seemed impossible to me before, given that I was blinded by my ignorance and anger. Now, I understood; the arguments with my mother began to thin out and dissolve suddenly, as if a heavy layer of ice had finally broken free and rejoined to flow in the water from which it had formed.

I not only had the desire to "cultivate" myself but also to understand myself, so I became passionate about psychology to better understand, in addition to my mother, my traumas. I was very struck by the reflections of Alice Miller. She was a Swiss psychologist and psychoanalyst known for her revolutionary studies on childhood traumas and the devastating effects of abuse and neglect on children. Her work profoundly influenced the field of child psychology and clinical psychology, leading to greater awareness and understanding of the underlying psychological processes affecting children's behavior and well-being. In particular, Alice Miller deeply explored the concept of the "true self" and the "false self" in relation to childhood traumas in her works. Here are some key points of her analyses:

- True Self and False Self: Miller argues that childhood traumas can lead to the creation of a "false self" in individuals. This false self is a mask that the person wears to fit the expectations and needs of parents or family, thus sacrificing their authenticity and emotional needs.
- Denial and Repression: According to Miller, children who experience trauma often have to deny their true feelings and needs to survive emotionally. This process of denial can lead to the creation of the false self, a person who acts in a conforming and adapted manner, but who internally suffers from conflicts and disconnection.
- Healing Process: Miller emphasized the importance of recognizing and addressing childhood traumas to allow the true self to emerge and heal. This process often involves deep therapeutic work to understand and integrate past traumatic experiences.
- Critique of Educational and Cultural Practices: Through her studies, Miller criticized educational and cultural practices that promote the denial of children's emotional

needs and the repression of their authentic expressions. She highlighted how such dynamics can perpetuate cycles of generational trauma.
- Social and Cultural Implications: Miller's analyses had significant implications in the field of psychology, suggesting that a more aware and compassionate society towards children's emotional needs can help prevent the perpetuation of childhood traumas.

I can say I was a child who tried to be "perfect", never to give my mother problems because I knew there were too many to face, so I find myself very much in Alice Miller's words. I had to lock my true self in a key for a long time - the one who wanted to cry, confide, scream, get angry - and I did a lot to build my "false self," or a girl who tried to give as few problems as possible and not to be annoying. In part it may be true, perhaps I felt "my mother's expectations" about me and I did not want to disappoint her, or it was an unconscious process that started with me, which was generated by childhood: "DO NOT BE LIKE HIM."

A Slow Healing Process

In 2006, when I was fifteen, there was the Court of Appeal's ruling regarding HIM, who had appealed against the 2003 sentence. The Court declared the appeal inadmissible but reduced the sentence to one year and nine months, with a one-month discount. At that time, I knew nothing about HIM and honestly, that was fine by me; there were no more updates, perhaps because my mother stopped following the trial or maybe she did, but chose not to inform us to avoid causing distress. I now know all these details because I've read all the documents, but back then my mind was occupied with other things.

I was trying to "heal" myself, to recover. So, I delved deeper into my readings, and thanks to my new school's philosophy teacher, I became passionate about the subject. My favorite philosophers were Nietzsche and Schopenhauer. I still remember a quote from the latter that deeply struck me: "Life is like a pendulum swinging between boredom and pain, passing through the brief and ephemeral interval of joy." In a kind of chain reaction, I managed to get my mother interested in reading too, which she confided she enjoyed a lot but had unfortunately neglected over the years due to all the situations caused by HIM. Another concept that made me reflect deeply was the passage where Schopenhauer described the three paths to escape from pain: art, ethics (or compassion), and asceticism. Schopenhauer believed that art was a means to temporarily elevate the individual from the prison of will. Through art, people can experience a state of pure contemplation, where the individual loses themselves in the artistic work and forgets personal desires and sufferings. Ethics, or compassion, is seen by Schopenhauer as a way to escape from suffering, as it allows individuals to recognize and share the pain of others. This recognition can alleviate personal suffering and create a bond of human solidarity. Lastly, asceticism: it is the most difficult path, representing the most radical and definitive escape from suffering. Through voluntary renunciation of desires and material needs, the individual can extinguish the will itself and reach a state of tranquility and liberation. I was so fascinated by his thoughts that I decided to include them in my high school thesis, which was on "Art Therapy." I found myself completely in his words and they helped me manage the pain.

I also expanded my musical interests, seeking ways to escape from pain. I found comfort in the desperate and sublime music and lyrics of REM, Radiohead, and especially Alice in Chains. At that time, I bought their unplugged album and played it repeatedly, initially causing apprehension for my mother. Eventually, even she, raised on Italian music from the 1960s, developed an interest in these artists, breaking a kind of "generational barrier" between us, which only strengthened our bond even more.

In 2009, there was a global event in the music world that struck the collective imagination of millions of people: Michael Jackson died. I was not his fan, but when he died, for some reason, I decided to listen to his lyrics and understand more about his life. I was amazed when I read about his childhood, with a violent father who forced him to perform, in order to "make money" thanks to his talent. I was even more amazed when I read that Michael Jackson had claimed to have forgiven his father because he was unaware of the actions he had done and the harm he had caused, as he himself had been a victim of violence. I kept wondering how it was possible to forgive such a father. Would I have been able to do it with mine?

In those years, my father was in prison. I found out one day when I received a letter from him from prison. He recounted that many years had passed between the sentence and the conviction; in the meantime, he had managed to rebuild his life, found a job, and was trying to live a "normal life." But then he was notified that he had to serve one year and nine months in prison. He wrote to me that this had turned his life upside down because he had changed in the meantime. I didn't believe for a moment that he had changed. On the contrary, I knew he would never change. I struggled to "empathize" with him and I didn't feel sorry at all that his life had been ruined: this was simply karma. I replied to the letter and was ruthless. I reminded him of all the harm he had done to me, highlighting that in my memory everything was still intact: I could not forget the pain he had caused to my family. I told him about the terrible consequences we had to endure, in constant economic precariousness and the psychological problems that HE had caused us. Of course, I replied to his final "I love you" with an "I hate you". There was a brief exchange of letters until I realized he had been released from prison. I didn't feel safe at all knowing that he was free again and I think neither did my mother.

At that time, my sister knew nothing, because she had moved to another region with her boyfriend. Relations between me and her were rather cold and even during our growth, unfortunately, we never got along. I believe this is due to one particular reason: once I read that in families where abuse or serious trauma occurs, there is a kind of "taboo" in talking about what happened. I think that's why we didn't bond much during our growth: each of us tried to free ourselves from memories of the past, but the past re-emerged every time we looked each other in the eyes. The lack of communication about what happened caused a deep misunderstanding between us, which we partly managed to heal many years later.

As for HIM, perhaps because I was inspired by the desire to "forgive," I finally decided to meet him. But in reality, thinking about it now, I did it for two specific reasons: my mother was drowning in debt, so I needed him to FINALLY give us some financial help; also, I wanted to see what I would feel seeing him in person. We met in a bar near our house, the scene of many tragedies. Seeing him again after so many years did not evoke anything positive. He hugged me but I remained as stiff as a piece of ice. Throughout the time, even when we sat down and he ordered coffee, I felt embarrassment, discomfort, and disgust. I observed him a lot and spoke little, just waiting for the moment of goodbye; HE, on the other hand, spoke a lot and probably expected a different, more docile and sweet attitude from me. But I was no longer a child. His face seemed even more stern, his expressionless and evil eyes hadn't changed, even though his words said otherwise. HE was my biggest nightmare and now seeing him materialized in front of me made me feel a strange effect: it brought my mind back to the bad memories of HIM and at the same time I wondered what memories I could build of HIM in the present. But I had no positive feelings, I felt trapped and just wanted to escape, like when I was a child in the car with HIM. When my mother asked me how it went, I replied: "It disgusted me, but at least he gave me some money and can be useful for something." I'm not ashamed to have thought that. After all he had done to us, my mother was in trouble because of him. I decided it was better to exploit him. In essence, I couldn't forgive him, but I wanted him to think so.

It was the summer of 2012 and I was on vacation with friends in Tuscany. When it was time to leave, my train had been canceled and I didn't have enough money for the return ticket. I called him for help. HE transferred me some money, but added: "you only call me for money, you never say I love you." At that point, I exploded. I vomited all my hatred on him, telling him that I would always hate him and that he would never see me again.

And so it was, until the following year. I never wanted to call HIM but I found myself forced to. It was summer and I was alone at home; my mother had gone to visit my sister. My beloved cat Milù was sixteen years old and not walking well: one evening she collapsed on the balcony and refused all my attempts to give her water or food. It was clear to me that she had chosen that place to die. I watched over her all night, and in the morning I realized she was dead. I cried for hours, I couldn't believe that she, an important part of my childhood and growth, was gone. Then I wondered what to do with her: I didn't have money to take her to a vet, nor could I bury her anywhere. So I called HIM. He arrived by car, with a woman; the exchange of words was brief and I gave him the bag in which I had placed Milù. I think this was the only compassionate gesture I have ever seen him make. Then I never heard or saw him again, until I was forced, once again, by an unexpected loss.

Meanwhile, my mother, burdened with debts up to her neck, was forced to sell the house, that house that had been the scene of our horrors and some brief moments of happiness. So we moved to another house, in a town in the Milan hinterland.

Young years and other Traumas
(2012 - 2024)

Processing Trauma

One day as an adult, I happened to scroll through Facebook as I often do. I came across a contact of mine who had shared the following lines from a book: "Today's non-fiction literature is filled with undisputed memories. Traumas are events that readers can access as they would enter a pavilion at an art or architecture Biennale; just buy a ticket and be ready to enjoy the aesthetic or intellectual experience. To the right, you can see the room where my mother and father fought furiously, while on the left, you can observe the courtyard where my schoolmates ridiculed me; finally, straight ahead, you will find the parking lot where my heart was broken by someone I loved, and on the upper floor, the highlight, the hospital room where a final farewell was said. My autobiography does not stop at any of these places because I cannot swear to have been there; I only have the impression of having passed through some of them with a pair of foggy lenses. If I did not severely force myself to say only what I know, I would reconstruct those moments like a Venice in Las Vegas, ugly and designed only for consumption. Instead, I want to rediscover the image of Roberta at twenty in an archive or in the memories of a witness [...]" (Giulia Scomazzon in "La paura ferisce come un coltello arrugginito").

Perhaps, being just an excerpt and not having read the book, I failed to grasp any irony that might have been behind these words, if there was any. I was hurt by these words, for reasons I cannot fully explain, but I will try.

First of all, because they tend to trivialize an experience that was mine and that of many others; secondly, because traumas are never the same as each other, and to group them all under a certain common denominator seems like a mathematical, sterile operation that does not take into account the sensitivity of the people involved in these traumatic experiences. Thirdly, because even if this were true and there was a tendency to "exhibit one's traumas" and if these followed similar paths, this writing does not take into account one fundamental thing: namely, it is not the trauma that defines a person, but how they seek to process, overcome, and face it. And I would also have a "fourth element": okay, there may be a common denominator among the traumas that many recount, but there are so many nuances in this common framework, it seems simplistic to sketch them in black and white.

For example, parents arguing may indeed be a classic: what makes a difference is how they argue, why the arguments happen, how they manifest, and what effect they have on witnesses of the argument. Do all parents, when arguing, throw their spouse against the wall? Do all parents vent their frustrations on their children, hitting or molesting them? Or is there a difference between a father who abandons his children, an absent father, or a violent father, even though all these different examples cause harm to those who suffer them? Someone who has experienced abandonment by a parent, whether father or mother, will develop a different trauma from someone who has experienced parental neglect and indifference; just as it will be different for someone who has experienced violence from one parent to another. Moreover, do all fathers, in this standard couple of arguing parents described by the author, end up in jail? Subsequently, in this phantom "common path," we have bullying. Is bullying always the same? So there is no difference between physical, verbal, psychological, or cyber bullying? And above all, do all victims of bullying react in the same way? Absolutely not.

There are bullied people who in turn become executioners, even ending up in mass murders, such as the prominent cases in the United States over the past decades, or they can become extremely insecure, shy, and lonely people. But not only that: there are bullied people who have not experienced family trauma, so they will definitely have a different outcome in their life; perhaps they will have low self-esteem, but having the support of their family is a different matter. Later, the author takes us to the "broken heart parking lot," after the first important relationship. Do all relationships begin and end in the same way, or are they all different and especially do those involved react according to their own nature? Absolutely yes. Finally, the last farewell that takes place in a hospital. This is the point that is most painful for me, because it is a wound that is still open and recent. Do all last farewells in hospitals happen in the same way? Do all family members of the person always have time to say goodbye? Or due to external factors - see Covid - can they not even go to visit their loved one who is dying forever? That's what happened to me. And in this "phantom" common path, I didn't just have to face the mourning of my mother, but also the unpleasant consequences that emerged after her death.

Another Sick Love

At this moment in the story, I will put HIM in the background to narrate another event that is nevertheless linked to what happened during childhood. Just as I read in Robin Norwood's book, "Women Who Love Too Much," I too ended up in the vortex of an unhealthy relationship, for the same reasons as my mother: I lacked self-esteem and had experienced a negative and aggressive father figure, which led me to seek out a similar male figure. That relationship lasted almost seven years, and sometimes I think about how much it stole my youthful years; just as my father had stolen my childhood. The person in question was a textbook narcissist, a manipulator, and was particularly verbally aggressive. Again, it was only years later that I read books to understand how this type of relationship works: at first, there is the so-called "love bombing," where the person overwhelms you with excessive compliments, attention, and love, just to trap you. Except you don't know you're prey, nor that theirs is a trap.

When we met in 2012, I was just twenty-one and he was thirty-eight. I was in an extremely fragile period of my life: despite making new friends, I felt I had no prospects, neither present nor future. After finishing high school, I couldn't afford to attend university due to perpetual financial difficulties. I couldn't find stable work, which caused me immense frustration. I suffered from generalized anxiety that prevented me from carrying out daily actions calmly, even just leaving the house. But I pushed myself to do it, and especially started traveling and attending concerts with my friends in Tuscany. It was there that a friend introduced me to S., who seemed to me like a pleasant guy. Unlike me, he was extroverted and easy-going, but he had a "dark side", like me, that I wanted to explore more.

What attracted me most was his story: he too had a difficult past and didn't hide it, but rather spoke about it immediately during our first meeting. His mother had him when she was very young, and his father abandoned him when he was little to start another family. Meanwhile, he grew up only with his mother, but she was nothing like mine: she was emotionally distant, aggressive, manipulative, and had serious mental issues. He said she forced him to do unthinkable things, like washing with cold water and disinfecting him, as if he "had something dirty inside" rather than just on the surface. Although his experience was different from mine, it made me empathize with him. Then, as mentioned before, came the love bombing, the constant compliments and praise, which made me fall into his trap. Once the fly is trapped in the web expertly woven by the "spider," it's hard to get out.

For the first three years, the relationship remained long-distance because he lived in Tuscany, so we saw each other occasionally. Then he moved to be with me in the province of Milan. At that time, I had found a job at an English school for children and, with my mother's help, rented a small studio where we could live together. He, seventeen years older than me and with plenty of work experience, would surely find a job, and together we would find a better, nicer, and bigger house to build a life together. That was the "plan": but making plans with a person like him was impossible. I realized that every piece I tried to build was knocked down by his arrogance, bullying, and narcissism. That initial love bombing turned into constant belittling of me. What I did was never enough, I was never enough. In reality, he did nothing. He found odd jobs here and there, mainly as a pet sitter; but aside from that, his activities were watching TV, drinking, and going to the supermarket to buy more to drink. He was a former addict and a heavy drinker: every time I tried to help him find work, for one reason or another he wouldn't go to interviews or they would go poorly because he presented himself badly. So I sank deeper into depression and despair. My mother, who initially viewed the relationship favorably - because, like all pathological narcissists, he initially presented himself in a benevolent light to convince people around him that he was a good person - then realized he wasn't what he had shown himself to be. She suffered greatly for me and tried to help me get out, but it wasn't easy due to his constant manipulation. Phrases like "you're worthless, you'll never find anyone but me, you're sick, who would ever want you? You're pitiful" were commonplace, especially in the evenings. Initially, I responded aggressively: I threw objects, shouted, and this only strengthened his ego. "See? You're crazy," he would say. So I decided on another strategy: ignore him and then respond calmly, assertively, and sharply. Every night we argued, for reasons unknown to me; and every night, without fail, he repeated those phrases. I began responding in a very petty and cynical manner. To his "you're worthless, you're not a real woman, you're disgusting, you make me sick," I calmly replied with statements like "I understand why your mother treated you like that, you're a horrible person." Initially, he didn't respond, but when he did, I ignored him, waiting for him to fall asleep, as alcohol eventually made him collapse and finally sleep. It often happened around dinner time. During those moments, I confided in my mother and she herself said, "finally, now you can breathe. We need to make a plan, you have to get out of there."

Why didn't I leave? Besides the reasons already mentioned, I was also afraid of what he might do - he had been violent with me only once, but I feared he might do it again once I left.

One evening, after yet another argument, I locked myself in the bathroom because I couldn't bear to hear him ranting in his alcoholic rambling. Then he started kicking the bathroom door many, many times while I blocked the door with my back. When I felt he had calmed down and opened it, he was kicking the door. The door slammed into me and particularly under my eye, causing a nasty wound. At that moment, I exploded with anger. I started kicking him, and I still feel ashamed of it, but I couldn't take it anymore. A few months later, after another argument in which he threw the cat at me over the plate where I was eating, I decided to leave immediately. We had two cats and I couldn't carry both: so I took the carrier and put Sid inside. I walked to the bus stop, but at that time - around 10 p.m. - no bus was coming; the next one was in an hour. In the meantime, he had followed me, shouting at me and trying to make me come back. But when I refused, he got angry and kicked the cat carrier, breaking it instantly. The cat ran away and narrowly escaped being hit by a car; I asked passersby for help, but no one stopped. I tried calling a taxi, but I was so upset that I couldn't find the right number, so I called the police and told them what happened. After that phone call, he disappeared. I was desperate because with the broken carrier, I didn't know how I would get my cat to safety. I called my mother crying and told her everything. "You did the right thing to leave, and don't worry about the cat, we'll look for him tomorrow, we'll find him," she said. Sid was in front of the bus stop, near a building with a garden: I saw him slip in there and prayed he would stay there until the next morning. Finally, the bus arrived and with a pounding heart, I watched Sid get farther away; I arrived at my mother's house in tears and she made me feel safe. She was sad for me, but mostly angry with him for what he had done to me. My mother could be as sweet as she was ruthlessly cruel to these people: the next morning he showed up at the bus stop to look for the cat. My mother gave him a murderous look and ignored him the entire time. The first day of searching went poorly and we couldn't find Sid.

I was in a bad situation because I had to go back to that house to get my things: as soon as I set foot there, I found the house completely destroyed. He said something like, "see, it's your fault that I did this, you could have just gone home, we would have fixed things, and Sid would still be here. You were despicable to call the police." In a fit of rage, I yelled back that it was only because of him that Sid had run away and that soon I would return to get Nancy, the other cat. I gathered my things and went to a nearby pet store to buy another carrier. He followed me again to the bus stop. He continued to insult me, and at that point did something unexpected: he spat in my face. I did the same, and the disgust I felt then, I still feel now. But it didn't end there. He got on the bus as well and in front of everyone started denigrating me, offending me, trying to portray me as a crazy person. I replied like this: "look, you're not credible, everyone sees you have a bottle inside your jacket at this hour in the morning, you're just a poor alcoholic." Everyone was watching and urged him to leave. A lady told me, "you're so sweet and a good girl, don't be with someone like him, leave him!" I replied, "thank you, that's what I did, the problem is that after I left him and went away, he kicked my cat and I'm forced to stay here to look for him."

Everyone looked at him with disdain, and finally he got off that damn bus. I hated those buses because if they had just come at the time I was leaving that evening, none of this would have happened. But in that moment, I felt good, as if I had been through a seven-year war and had won a historic battle. We found Sid two days later, and that was the happiest moment of my life that I can remember, at that time.

And slowly, after a long journey, I found myself again.

A New Life

I went into therapy because, in addition to the childhood traumas I had partly worked through, this new trauma had emerged that needed addressing. My father, who throughout this ordeal only appeared with a few messages on my birthday, became the focal point of my entire therapeutic journey. I went to see Dr. L. R., who followed me for about two years. She certainly helped me process the recent trauma with my ex and taught me strategies to manage anxiety, like diaphragmatic breathing, for instance. People with anxiety tend to breathe from the upper chest, as if something truly tragic is happening and our breath becomes short, alarmed. Well, an anxious person always breathes like that, even when just walking down the street. She taught me to breathe from the lower belly and to adopt this type of breathing to calm anxiety; it worked. Additionally, she used cognitive-behavioral therapy with me to help manage some of my phobias, such as riding public transportation. I don't know why they had always caused me anxiety; maybe because close contact with people was a sore point for me, or maybe because I felt trapped inside those "boxes," whether underground on the subway or above ground on trains and buses. My biggest fear was the subway, and what I did to combat the anxiety was to tuck myself into a corner, turning my back on everyone to avoid their stares. "Do you know that in doing this, rather than avoiding stares, you actually attract them?"

my therapist said to me one day. "No, I hadn't thought about it." "Yes, it's one of those protective traps that make us feel safe, but only perpetuate our anxiety." "And how?" "See, if you feel the need to tuck into a corner, it means you're trying to protect yourself from something, so your anxiety increases. If instead you try to sit or turn the other way, you'll see there's nothing you need to defend against, and your anxiety will subside." I put these tips into practice, and at first it was difficult; but little by little, I noticed she was right, my anxiety decreased. In addition to this, I had to manage my separation from my ex. Separating from a pathological narcissist is not at all simple: S. continued to bombard me with messages and calls; I admit I didn't manage to definitively cut off all communication with him, as I should have done. Because now that the fly was free to fly, the spider tried in every way to bring her back to him, once again a prisoner of his web, made of manipulations, humiliations, and degradation. Even my mother helped me a lot during that period: she was happy that I had freed myself from him; I had returned to living a "normal" life. That's something I had always missed in life, "normalcy"; but at that moment, I found it again. I could appreciate the pleasure of taking a hot shower that lasted more than a minute - there was almost never hot water in that "house." Besides the "privilege" of making myself a coffee in two minutes - over there, I had induction hobs instead of gas that took a long time to heat up. And I also rediscovered that "mundane" pleasure of having a washing machine: in the other house, I didn't have one and was forced to shuttle back and forth to my mother's house. In 2019, I found a job as a school educator, and it was a new experience for me; in the meantime, my mother helped me continue my studies. My dream had always been to attend university, but I couldn't afford it. With that new job and her help, I managed to start studying for a degree in Education Sciences and Training. My "father" never helped me, not even with this. Later, he would say to me, "It was you - meaning my sister and I - who drained your mother's money." But this is a point I'll address later on. It wasn't easy to balance work and study, and I admit the former caused me quite a bit of stress, but it was also very stimulating. My task was to help children and teenagers, mainly from middle schools, who had Specific Learning Disabilities (SLD) or behavioral disorders such as ADHD and Oppositional Defiant Disorder (ODD). I helped them manage their behavior in class and organize their assignments; but not only that. I often became their confidant, like a kind of "big sister." Many of them had a troubled history: family, economic, psychological hardships. Despite the difficulty of the work, I managed to put myself in their shoes, and helping them made me feel good: I felt I had found my vocation, helping others - perhaps because I couldn't help myself, or perhaps because it also helped me to "heal." In this regard, at the end of therapy, I asked my psychotherapist if she could write me a report documenting my disorders. I asked for this because of something that happened later on, when there was an intention to sue my father for the psychological damage we suffered - although all lawyers advised against it, as the offenses were time-barred.

The report was as follows:

Assago, June 15, 2022

The undersigned Dr. L. R., as Psychologist and Psychotherapist [...] certifies that Desirèe Gullo, born in Milan on 24/07/91, came to my practice for a psychotherapy journey. Based on the psychological assessment, a diagnosis of Social Anxiety Disorder and Major Depressive Disorder was formulated. The diagnosis emerged from clinical interviews and direct observation of behavior. The social anxiety problem associated with depressive disorder is characterized by the following symptoms: marked and persistent fear related to social situations; fear of judgment; discomfort in social situations; tachycardia; tremors; muscle tension; depressed mood; weight loss; marked decrease in interest and pleasure in activities; insomnia; lack of energy; feelings of worthlessness; inappropriate guilt feelings; recurrent thoughts of death; recurrent suicidal ideation. The symptoms cause clinically significant distress with impairment in social and occupational functioning. The problem is not attributable to the physiological effects of a substance or general medical condition. From the patient's history, the etiopathogenesis of the disorder clearly emerged, caused by long exposure to traumatic events. The patient has indeed suffered abuse from the paternal figure and witnessed episodes of domestic violence against her mother and older sister. The pathological environment of childhood abuse forces the minor to be trapped in a place where she must struggle to maintain a sense of trust in people, security in a treacherous environment, control in a situation of absolute unpredictability. Chronic abuse occurred in a family climate of pervasive terror, characterized by threats of death.

Pandemic and Lockdown

When Covid arrived and the subsequent lockdown began, I was living with my mother. I had just started working at school when the epidemic broke out in March 2020. I can't remember the exact moment the lockdown was declared, but I vividly recall the first time I had to wear a mask: I felt a lot of shame, though I'm not sure why. Before going to the supermarket, I would peer from the balcony and invariably see a long line of people waiting to enter. Not everyone could enter at once, and initially, you couldn't go in pairs, so my mother and I took turns. Both of us were working from home, and the situation became quite stressful: I hadn't received instructions on how to conduct myself, as my job required in-person presence. So every day, I would video call the students to talk to them or help them with their assignments. Often, they wouldn't answer or there would be communication and connection issues. In short, it was not easy at all. Meanwhile, my mother had been given a company laptop and worked in the other room.

My mother and I have always had a great relationship, but I admit she was an overprotective mother, and our bond was somewhat symbiotic. The lockdown certainly didn't make things easier, even though we got along well. But I felt that, after this experience, I needed to try to become more independent from her. So I decided to rent a house once that devastating period was over.

When the lockdown finally ended, I decided to take a trip with some friends. It was during this trip that one of them introduced me to a guy, Daniele. In September 2021, I returned to school, and we all wore masks. The school environment itself was suffocating, but with masks, it became almost unbearable. During the first wave, we all anxiously followed the daily bulletin of deaths, which one day exceeded 900. At that time, the vaccine was not yet available. With the arrival of the second wave, cases in schools began to rise again, often forcing us teachers and educators to stay at home. Meanwhile, my mother received bad news from her company: there was going to be a sale to another company, resulting in hundreds of layoffs. In fact, half of her colleagues were let go. She got early retirement, so she was luckier. The first vaccines began to circulate, and for some reason, my mother got scared: she had heard of cases where the vaccine had caused health damage.

I tried to make her understand that, in reality, from what I had read, those cases were very few, but she wouldn't listen to reason: "I'm not getting vaccinated." It was as if the roles had reversed: as her daughter, I tried everything to convince my mother to get vaccinated, as she probably did with us when we were little. From this experience, I understood that parents can sometimes be more stubborn than their children. "Do it for your health," I kept telling her. She replied, "It's precisely for my health that I don't want the vaccine." Until I said to her, "Mom, do you realize that if you don't get vaccinated and something happens to you, then you'll leave me alone?" Maybe only then did she hesitate slightly. "No, what are you saying? Nothing will happen to me."

Meanwhile, the Green Pass arrived: to work and enter public places, vaccination was mandatory. So I got vaccinated and then the subsequent boosters.

The following summer, the situation with infections seemed to have decreased, so we had more freedom to go out, although gatherings were still prohibited. I started seeing Daniele, the friend who had been introduced to me. I had tried to ask him out several times, but for one reason or another, he always gave me the slip. I was really frustrated with the situation, and one day while walking with my mother, I confided in her. She replied with a sentence that, in hindsight, surprised me. "I am convinced that you two will be together; it may not be now, maybe in a few months or a year, but it will happen." My mother's prophecy came true; it's a pity she didn't have the same intuition about her health.

In October 2021, Daniele and I were already a stable couple and still are. He was completely different from my ex, and that's what attracted me to him: he was kind, gentle, shy, and respectful. We could talk about everything, and that amazed me: I wasn't used to that with my ex, where every conversation had to be carefully weighed to avoid angering him. With Daniele, everything was simpler, spontaneous, natural. NORMAL. Nothing like that narcissistic, egocentric, manipulative being—and I could go on indefinitely. My mother was happy with the news. "See, I knew that sooner or later it would happen; it's impossible for a guy not to want to be with you!" She had this very high opinion of me, probably common to all mothers towards their daughters, but I don't think it applies to everyone. For her, I was this creature so good, beautiful, kind who deserved to have what had been taken away from her: happiness. Not because of this did she not see my flaws, indeed, but she managed not to make them weigh on me or emphasize them with the delicacy that only she had had towards me. I would have liked to have had this opinion of myself too.

I didn't get to introduce Daniele to my mother because she contracted Covid a month later, in December, after going to visit my sister for Christmas. A few days later, she took the test and tested positive: from that moment on, I saw my mother only through the screen of my cell phone. The last time I heard her voice was on January 14, 2022. I remember this date well because she was not feeling well at all: somehow, I sensed that it would be our last phone call. I remember asking her, "If you could go back, would you get vaccinated?" She looked pale and tired, struggling to speak. She said, uncertainly, "I don't know, yes, maybe..."

That same evening, she was admitted to San Paolo Hospital; they put on the oxygen helmet, as Covid protocols required. My uncle informed me of this because my mother managed to send him a message and even a photo of herself with the helmet. My uncle told me that she didn't warn me that evening because she didn't want to worry me, as I had to go to work the next day. Then her condition worsened: she was transferred to the Intensive Care Unit of San Carlo Hospital; from that moment on, she was no longer conscious. That period at work was dominated by terrible anxiety, which I tried to manage by talking about the situation with those around me: parents of the children, teachers, janitors, students. Once, a mother of a child I was helping told me, "Look, it's nothing, it's like having the flu. You'll see, she'll be fine."

I couldn't visit her; no one was allowed to visit their sick loved ones. The doctors updated us on her health almost daily until one day they told us they would allow us to visit our mother because she wouldn't survive the night. They let us into the ward: it was me, my sister, and my uncle. Before entering the room, they made us put on heavy, white suits with gloves. We looked like astronauts, just landed on an unknown planet. Seeing my mother lying on that bed, intubated, caused me a terrible feeling, as if my life had ended there, along with hers. Her body, once soft, and her round face seemed now drained, tired of fighting. My sister cried desperately, saying something like "Mom, don't leave us, we love you." I cried too but said nothing, perhaps just "I love you." I knew she was gone by then, and that would be the last time we saw her. It was the worst day of my life.

The day my mom died

On January 31, 2022, the most traumatic event of my life occurred: my mother passed away in the Covid intensive care unit at San Carlo Hospital in Milan. By some strange twist of fate, her death date coincided with my boyfriend's birthday. With her, a part of me departed. My sister, other relatives, and I were in a state of confusion and shock that I still struggle to process today.
I took bereavement leave from work, which, per my contract, was only three days. Three days to mourn my mother and organize the funeral felt like an insult. A few days later, my uncles accompanied me to the funeral agency, where we discovered that my parents were only legally separated and not divorced. Therefore, my mother was still legally married. The agency owner informed me that I needed to call my father to obtain his signature and consent for the funeral, as he was still legally her husband. Those words sent shivers down my spine.

I asked my aunt to call him because I wasn't mentally prepared. I heard he was devastated by the news and wanted to speak with me, but I refused. Later on, HE sent his documents and signature via message to my phone. I informed my sister, who couldn't be there as she lived far from Lombardy; she screamed and cried in despair because the monster she thought we had buried had resurfaced. Naturally, he wasn't invited to the funeral.

We decided not to hold a church ceremony and instead opted to cremate my mother, as she had never been religious. Present were her colleagues and friends, my relatives, myself, and my boyfriend. My sister gave a poignant speech, recalling the funny moments about her; I couldn't bring myself to speak.

I decided to terminate my lease and return to my mother's house. Thus began the period of paperwork: loans to settle, the mortgage to extinguish. There was no time to grieve, although tears inevitably flowed freely. First and foremost, we needed to obtain the death certificate - and I discovered that bureaucracy stops for nothing. Many documents were required, including her medical records. It took a month to obtain them: a file spanning 500 pages. The death certificate was needed by the bank to settle the loans and mortgage on the house, which we had believed would be extinguished with the policy. Meanwhile, university exams loomed: I remember having one just a month after her passing, an English exam. I don't know how, but I found the strength to take it, scoring top marks. I felt I had to continue giving my best because she had made so many sacrifices to allow me to study.

Going to work was the most difficult thing of all: I couldn't bear the weight of the gazes that "knew." I could no longer keep my problems locked away in a securely closed drawer, as I had done before. Now that drawer was overflowing, and I couldn't keep it closed: a wave of bureaucratic debris was engulfing me like a flood, impossible to contain. I struggled to manage the bureaucratic aspects of mourning alongside work: I had to take days off to go to the bank, to lawyers, to the revenue agency. My employers were not pleased. One day, I made an appointment at the bank to request authorization to pay my mother's funeral expenses from her account. I entered, and the clerk asked to see my green pass. It was only then that I realized it had expired the day before. "I'm sorry, but I can't let you in. Please make another appointment after you've renewed your green pass," she said. At that point, I burst into tears. "Please, I came to pay for my mother's funeral expenses, please let me in." Fortunately, the clerk showed compassion and allowed me to proceed.

Because of all these permissions, they started accusing me of not being diligent enough in my work because I was absent too often - this, just a month after my mother's death. Even the mother of a child I cared for complained about me, the same one who had told me, "It's just a flu, she'll recover." I decided to take a break from work: it was impossible to manage everything and not lose my mind. There were also her things to pack away, the photos, her personal belongings, the documents. We had to figure out what to keep, what to throw away. It was a terrible moment.
But that wasn't the worst: when we found out that he, as her "spouse," was entitled to a third of her assets and the widow's pension, it was another blow. Fate, or rather the law, had dealt us another wound.

The Inheritance (or The Dissection)

This is what we discovered when my sister and I contacted the first lawyer. We believed that after the court sentence against HIM, he had lost all inheritance rights regarding my mother. However, the lawyer needed to review the trial and appeal sentences to verify this. We didn't have them—they must have been lost in the move or who knows where—so, since everything wasn't digitalized back then, the lawyer had to go to the court archive to obtain them. But even this had long waiting times.

After about a month, he finally obtained the sentences and emailed me copies. I went to his office with my boyfriend, convinced that my father had no rights over my mother after his conviction.

"See, on the last page, it says he loses inheritance rights toward the victim, so he can't inherit from my mother, right?" I asked, confident that I was correct.

"Actually, no. It says he lost inheritance rights regarding you and your sister, not your mother."

"And why didn't he lose them concerning her?"

"Because the law only provides for loss of rights in cases of harassment, not domestic violence."

"But isn't there any law that could declare him unworthy of inheriting from my mother, given the conviction?"

"Yes, there is, but first of all, the statute of limitations has expired. And the law on unworthiness states that someone is declared unworthy if they kill the spouse, attempt to alter a will by force, or make threats." "Is there nothing we can do to challenge this?" "No, your mother should have kept the process alive through her lawyer; that way, the statute of limitations wouldn't have expired. But over twenty years have passed."

I was shocked by everything he said; I couldn't believe it. When I read Article 463 of the Civil Code on unworthiness to inherit, I felt anger and disgust because it didn't at all consider the loss of inheritance rights for those who committed crimes—other than murder—against the spouse.

Article 463 - Causes of Unworthiness

A person is excluded from inheritance as unworthy:
- Anyone who has deliberately killed or attempted to kill the person whose succession is in question, their spouse, a descendant, or an ascendant, unless there is a cause for non-punishment under criminal law.
- Anyone who has committed, against one of these people, an act to which criminal law applies the provisions on homicide.
- Anyone who has falsely accused or reported one of these people for a crime punishable by life imprisonment or imprisonment for not less than three years if there was an irrevocable conviction.
- Anyone who has testified against the person whose succession is in question, accused of a crime punishable as

mentioned in the previous number, if there was an irrevocable conviction.
- Anyone who has fraudulently or violently induced the person whose succession is in question to make, revoke, or change the will, or has prevented its formation, revocation, or change.
- Anyone who has suppressed, falsified, or altered the will by which the succession would be regulated.
- Anyone who has created a false will or knowingly used one.

Only recently did I think of consulting legislation on this matter in other European countries. I discovered that the provisions on unworthiness to inherit vary significantly. I focused on two countries in particular:

- In Germany, the Civil Code (Bürgerliches Gesetzbuch, BGB) provides for unworthiness to inherit for those who have committed a serious crime against the spouse or a person who would have inherited, including domestic violence crimes.
- In Spain, the Civil Code provides for unworthiness to inherit for those who have committed acts of domestic violence against the spouse.

In Italy, there is absolutely no provision on this matter. My disgust for this situation kept growing.

Meanwhile, during my now-daily correspondence with the bank, I discovered that in bureaucratic terms, the deceased is referred to as "de cuius." One day, I read an email from the bank where my mother was referred to in this way. It was the first time I had heard this term; it took me a few minutes to realize they were referring to her. It was all so clinical and impersonal, cold, like I imagine an autopsy room to be. My mother was there, dissected in every part: "Here's the limb of her bank assets, there's the amputated leg of the deceased's loans, over there we need to cut with a scalpel to settle the mortgage." Oh no, it's not over yet; there's also HIM to "strip the carcass."

It seemed that this lexical operation was a horrible attempt to remove any human and emotional connotation from my mother. As if she was no longer a person, not even a dissected body, but a "problematic" customer code in their system. My sister and I managed to settle her loans with difficulty, but the mortgage was a completely different situation. As we already knew, my mother had taken out a life insurance policy, so in case of death, the mortgage would be settled. Instead, we discovered that even though my mother had paid for that policy, it was never activated. My sister and I spent entire days organizing all our mother's documents until we managed to gather them all. We consulted the lawyer and handed over all documents related to the policy, the mortgage, the house, and he saw the proof that the policy had been taken out. But the bank continued to claim that it had never been applied.

So, not only had my mother BEEN CHEATED BY THE BANK because they hadn't activated the policy, but she had also BEEN CHEATED BY THE STATE, which gave a third of her inheritance and her pension to her old TORMENTOR. Despite everything he had done, my "father" was declared worthy of her inheritance and her pension. And the law didn't allow us to do anything to prevent it. It was as if the law was on HIS side. In fact, this was one of the phrases HE wrote to me later.

The lawyer told us that there was a way to prevent him from taking part of the inheritance: he could renounce it. But to me and my sister, this seemed impossible: for HIM to show a shred of humanity, compassion; to finally show remorse for what he had done and try to redeem himself to come even remotely close to what he should have been, that is, a good father? IMPOSSIBLE. So, despite already knowing it was a lost battle, I reestablished contact with him.

I knew my father had started another family and had a child with another woman. At first, I asked him to renounce the inheritance, and after much hesitation, he was about to accept. However, my sister and I didn't know that having a child changed everything. The lawyer clarified the situation for us.

"If he refuses the inheritance, it automatically passes to the child. Since the child is a minor, the matter would go to the Court, which has to determine whether this inheritance can pass to the child or not. The problem is that this would lengthen the succession process, thus jeopardizing all the other matters."

"How can the inheritance pass to the child if this child isn't even my mother's biological child?" I wondered to myself. But by then, I had learned not to ask too many logical questions: I had come to understand that the law was beyond any logic.

I don't remember the exact reason why the lawyer told us the matter was too complex and that he didn't handle successions, so we had to find another lawyer. I consulted several who I asked, besides about the mortgage issue, if it was possible to prevent him from being an heir, but they all answered the same way.

"Nothing can be done, the statute of limitations has expired, they were legally married because they weren't divorced, the law allows this."

The Petition

So, I decided to write a petition to change the law, particularly the one regarding unworthiness to inherit. Unexpectedly, the owner of the platform contacted me and said this petition would have media power. He and his collaborators helped me rewrite it and find an appropriate hashtag to launch it on social media: "#MOLESTATO." I launched it on May 31, 2022, and so far, we have obtained more than seventy-seven thousand signatures.
The text reads as follows:

"I am a 30-year-old woman, my name is Desirée, and this is the story of an injustice that still haunts us after years; it is, in fact, a story of one injustice after another.
My mother separated from my father in 1998, following domestic violence and sexual harassment against her and us, her two daughters, Desirée and Simona. The trial lasted many years, during which my mother unfortunately accumulated debt, as lawyers are expensive and trials are long. She struggled greatly, being alone with two daughters.
In 2003, my 'father' was sentenced to 3 years in prison, plus compensation for the moral, physical, and psychological damages he caused my mother, my sister, and me. The compensation amounted to 36,000 euros (12,000 euros for each of the injured parties). Additionally, this sentence resulted in the loss of his

parental rights and inheritance rights, but only concerning us, not our mother. We never received the compensation money. Over the years, we did not know that we needed to send a letter to keep the process alive (which later became statute-barred, so now he is no longer obliged to pay damages).

In 2008, there was an appeal, and my father also received a pardon, reducing his sentence to 1 year. However, we received none of the compensation money. During these years, my mother was also forced to sell the house she had bought in Milan, thanks to her job (she worked for Sma, which became Auchan and now Conad), because she was overwhelmed by debt.

Over the years, however, she managed to pay off most of her debts and finally retired, despite the transfer of her company (Auchan) to Conad, which resulted in many layoffs, but she managed to get early retirement.

On January 31, 2022, however, we were struck by another tragedy: the death of my mother from COVID-19.

Following her death, my sister and I thought we were the only heirs. Instead, there was also my father. We discovered that since they were only separated and not divorced (my mother could not afford to pay for the divorce), legally, it was as if they were still 'married.'

So, adding insult to injury: he was also an heir, and despite having committed acts of violence against my mother, my father receives her survivor's pension of 900 euros and will inherit, meaning he will be entitled to my mother's estate, which consists of the property she had later purchased, with a mortgage still to be paid off.

After everything he did, how is it possible that the sentence did not foresee the loss of his inheritance rights regarding my mother? Why was there no automatic divorce after the series of crimes he committed? And why isn't time given to minors, once grown, to be compensated if this was never done?

For all these reasons, I ask you to sign this petition. It is unfair that there are no rules to protect those who have been victims of violence, even if adjudicated, so I ask for:

- Extending the time to appeal for those who suffered violence as minors;
- Automatic divorce for separated women who are victims of domestic violence;
- In cases where the couple is separated but not divorced, automatic loss of all inheritance rights for those who committed domestic violence against the spouse, especially if minors are involved in the violence;
- Including a new article in the law on unworthiness to inherit, declaring 'unworthy to inherit a person who has committed acts of domestic violence against the deceased spouse, with a final criminal sentence.'

These rules must also be applied retroactively for all those who have been unable to obtain justice.

Thank you to those who will support me."

This petition sparked the interest of some journalists. The platform owner asked for my permission to give my number for interviews. Initially, there was one journalist, then two more followed. So, I saw my face and story in various newspapers: Today.it, Fanpage, and many national dailies reported the news from Repubblica to Il Corriere della Sera. But what I never expected was to end up on TV. One thing I was certain of in my life before then was that I would never become someone who appeared in front of a camera; I was never one of those people who wanted to be seen at all costs, quite the opposite. And I never thought the spotlight would shine on me for such a terrible reason. But for a brief period, I had those "fifteen minutes of fame," as Andy Warhol famously said, predicting that in the future, everyone would have the spotlight thanks to the media. Unlike many, I didn't desire that "fame": I did it for my mother and to get her the justice she deserved. She fought for us, and I couldn't do anything but fight for her; I felt that was the only way to be heard.

A presenter from a TV channel called me to talk about my story: it was a live broadcast. I temporarily forgot my anxiety about appearing and prepared myself. The show featured two lawyers; one of them contacted me, offering to help us for free. Subsequently, two more newsrooms contacted me.

One day, a cameraman, a sound engineer, and a journalist from Studio Aperto crossed the threshold of my mother's house. They asked me questions about my story, about her, and about HIM. I tried not to cry while they filmed me and some photos of her. However, the interviewer from Le Iene did not appreciate my composure.

My 15 Minutes of Fame

Before continuing with the interviews, I need to take a step back and talk about the legal matters. The second lawyer, who had offered to help us for free, was initially very supportive. However, after a few months, he proved to be negligent, not responding to our messages and not following our case. During this time, negotiations were ongoing - which lasted several months - between HIS lawyers and ours. We had proposed to let HIM have the money from my mother's account on the condition that he renounced the money from the house sale, but after taking his time and keeping us in suspense, he refused.

One day, I received a letter from the bank recognizing the retroactivity of the policy my mother had taken out on the mortgage. This meant we could pay off the mortgage, but the situation required urgent action. I wrote to the lawyer, without getting a response. Realizing that her goal was to appear on TV - in fact, Le Iene had contacted her too, and she was going to appear on air - I decided to cut ties with her and look for a third lawyer. The second lawyer was very angry, I think because she would no longer appear on TV in that broadcast.

Months passed between one interview and another. I had moved near Pavia with my boyfriend. Nina's crew asked me if the house in question, the subject of the dispute, was where I was living. This interview was the most emotionally challenging. I tried to suppress my emotions, but when I burst into tears, Nina said: "Finally! It seemed like I was talking to a police officer." To me, it felt like an interrogation. I didn't want to appear suffering; I wanted HIM to feel ashamed. After an hour of questions, they left. The segment aired many months later, reduced to about ten minutes. In the segment, they also showed the moment when they found my father and asked him why he wouldn't renounce the inheritance. He did not answer.

Thanks to the third lawyer, we managed to resolve the mortgage issue, though it wasn't fully paid off. My mother's account was used to pay the difference, depleting it. At the bank, we had to declare that the division would be for the three heirs. The bank employees showed us support and disgust for him and the whole situation. What I appreciate most of all was the support from people: especially the seventy-seven thousand people who signed the petition, commented on the interviews, and shared similar stories. Some suggested that just getting a divorce would have avoided all this. But that doesn't change the fact that the law on unworthiness is flawed: the spouse who commits serious crimes against the deceased spouse should be excluded from the inheritance.

Although the third lawyer resolved the mortgage and policy situation, unfortunately, she was not helpful with this other issue - and I admit I felt a lot of disgust and disappointment. But by then,

I was used to it. When I asked her what could be done to address that "legal loophole," if we could take any legal action, she responded like this: "There is no legal loophole; if the law was made this way, it was the will of the legislators." Exactly what you want to hear from your lawyer, who in theory, should be on your side. So, I asked: "Okay, it may be so. But my will is to obtain justice. Can't we do anything to sue him, to claim moral damages?"

"I advise you to put this matter aside, to think about your life, your future."

I felt completely disillusioned and abandoned by those who should have defended me. I even tried to contact some politicians, without any expectations. One of them replied, writing that it was necessary to propose a law on the matter. But after this message, she no longer responded to my follow-ups and requests to understand what I should do.

The "Grieving" Widower

I feel it is necessary to dedicate a final chapter to HIM, who seems to be the beginning and end of all things - as if he were God coming down to Earth. Unfortunately, in light of the facts, it is so: my father has been treated by the law as a poor "grieving" widower, who needed my mother's survivor's pension to console himself from the terrible affliction of grief. Now he can dry his tears with my mother's money. Thank you, ITALIAN STATE.

During the initial stages with our first lawyer, I consulted his criminal record and discovered several things I was unaware of: for example, he used to steal cars and then register them in my mother's name. For this, she was accused in court but fortunately acquitted. My mother didn't even have a driver's license. I found out he was convicted of aggravated assault, drug offenses, dealing, fraud, and then the icing on the cake that fell on us. I wonder how it is possible to "reward" such a person with my mother's pension.

Now, I want to focus on our post-mortem relationship, which followed rather bipolar phases. At first, the widower was truly grieving. Even the hardest hearts would melt at the news of the death of the mother of your children. Then, something else must have clicked in his mind: like a shark smelling blood, he smelled the scent of money and could not resist the call. It's not that my mother had a great fortune - also because, due to him and the legal matter, he had eaten away everything she had - but recently, my mother was doing quite well, even financially. Only, she still had many loans to pay off, contracted following the whole affair.

In some exchanges we had - mainly through messages and Whatsapp voice notes - he said many things that I still struggle to digest. I am well aware that I did not act rationally: I should have kept calm, but the anger towards him and for that situation was a fire that could not be extinguished in any way. In fact, if at first my tones were "neutral" and so were his, they eventually became bitter and spiteful, because I couldn't accept that he did nothing to redeem himself. And so he finally revealed himself for what he was: a person who was not in the least repentant of what he had done; in fact, the most serious thing is that I believe that even today HE thinks he did nothing wrong. His voice, I believe, is one of the most annoying things I have ever heard in my life: that cold tone, as if it came not from a human being but from something else; that arrogance of someone who knows that people like him will always win, would have been intolerable for anyone. And I could not help but associate that voice with the one who yelled when we were little, the one who dared to say "I love you" and at the same time told us "I will kill you." I managed to pick up in his voice that old disdain he used towards my mother, for example when he mocked, humiliated, and beat her, in front of me. I deleted all his messages, but I still remember some of them. Those in which I urged him to give up my mother's money, to redeem himself after all he had done, and where he replied, verbatim: "I'm at work, stop your crap." And how can I forget that time he wrote to me, regarding my petition, "the law will never change, and even if it does, it will be in twenty years." But what I remember most, and of which I still have the recorded audio, is when I called him, after he replied to one of my messages: "you two have eaten the money from her account."

I find it hard to listen to this recording again, but I think it's useful to understand the abominable psychology of the character.

"Hi. How dare you say that we two have eaten from our mother's account, why do you think so?"

"Eh... Because I think so. Because that's how it is, the accounts don't add up."

"But what do you know about the life we lived? Because of you, we had a shitty life, my mother went into debt to pay the lawyers."

"Yes, but the accounts don't add up... You know, now we have to deal with the accounts and divide the money..."

"Why do you talk about things you don't know about?"

"Eh, for example, your sister's car that she paid for..."

"Right, because according to you, if a daughter needs help paying for the car, it means she's eating from the account? Do you realize what you're saying? You talk when you were supposed to compensate us and didn't give us anything!"

"Still with this story, you keep bringing it up…"

"No, I'm not bringing up anything, these are just the facts."

"I've already paid."

"No, you haven't paid. You did jail time, but you never compensated us."

"That's enough now."

"Do you have a conscience? How do you look at yourself in the mirror?"

"Look, I'm looking in the mirror right now. Eh, it looks like I don't have a conscience."

"Have you ever wondered what you put your daughters through?"

"Yes, I've wondered."

"And then don't dare to say those things, we had no money to eat, you don't know a damn thing about our lives, got it?"

"Yes, okay. Then I'll leave you alone, so you can vent by yourself."

"I'll leave you to be a kept man. The only thing you're capable of doing."

"Yes, only you worked."

"You're a parasite, and you dare to be cocky with me?"

"I'm not being cocky, and you're offending me."

"No, I'm just stating the facts. If you're not man enough to accept them, ask yourself some questions."

"You ask yourself some questions too."

"I do ask myself questions, but my conscience is clear."

The call ends more or less like this, with him blabbering "yes yes, okay it's clear that I don't have a conscience, bye-bye." I don't know if he ever had a conscience, but I believe that such a person should be eradicated from humanity.

Nolite Te Bastardes Carborundorum

We were like small Davids fighting an impregnable monster: my sister, my uncles, my boyfriend, and I against Goliath - JUSTICE, HIM, THE BANKS, THE LAW.

I had believed, deep down, that things would turn out well. I believed in the childish vision of "and they lived happily ever after," in the rhetoric of "the good will triumph over the bad," despite being a cosmic pessimist by nature, like Leopardi. In my head, there was a mantra I repeated to myself: "It is not possible that JUSTICE will do nothing, that it will not be on our side." But ONCE AGAIN, we were defeated.

One day, another newsroom contacted me. They asked if I wanted to participate in a program where women victims of violence told their stories as "survivors." I, very bitterly, replied that I did not feel like it because we were not "survivors," we had been "defeated."

"Nolite te bastardes carborundorum" means "don't let the bastards grind you down." It is the reason I decided to tell my story and my mother's. This phrase is found in "The Handmaid's Tale" by Margaret Atwood, from which a famous TV series was made. Watching it with my boyfriend, I couldn't help but empathize with the protagonist, June. They had taken everything from her: her life, her husband, her daughter, even her name. They had enslaved, tortured, and beaten her, to make her a handmaid in that dystopian world where infertility was the plague that infested the world, and the state of Gilead had seized these fertile women to serve as "incubators" for other women.

I lived in another dystopian world: where abusive and molesting fathers get the inheritance and pension of the woman they mistreated. Despite the spotlight from newspapers and television, no one did anything to prevent this from happening: it would have been enough to insert a small clause in an outdated law written in the 1950s. Instead, on July 19, 2023, a few days before my birthday, we signed the sale of my mother's house in front of the notary. The proceeds were divided into three: my sister, HIM, and me. To the daughters of the deceased and the "spouse" who molested them. But who cares, after all, they are now time-barred offenses! My response to this phrase, uttered by all the great lawyers I consulted, is this: the crimes may be time-barred, but the pain has not expired, the psychological, emotional, and economic damage he caused us has not expired, and above all, the expiration does not mean that the events did not happen. This further injustice only increases my disillusionment with the ITALIAN LAW and JUSTICE that allowed this disgrace.

The only satisfaction for me, knowing I had lost this battle, was to make him suffer. So, for the entire time we were there in front of the notary, I did not give him a glance. Not even when he said "hello" at the beginning; I continued up the stairs without saying anything and without ever looking at him. I wanted him to feel small and insignificant like a cockroach. This was my bitter and pathetic revenge, the only possible one, because the State and the Law had prevented me from having my rightful revenge: that he be totally excluded from everything and not get a penny. I wanted him to feel like shit receiving that money and maybe I succeeded. But there remains the aftertaste of an injustice that will never be avenged by anyone.

I still want to believe that the "bastards will not grind me down," I still want to believe that one day I will be the one to do it: but in the end, what remains is a bitter defeat. I lost. We all lost from this affair: the Italian State lost its credibility once again; the Law lost because it protected the perpetrators and not the victims once again; women lost because their rights were trampled once again.

But I am tired of losing. And I am still angry. I am still waiting for that moment when I can finally serve that "cold dish" of revenge; rather of JUSTICE.

And you?

Acknowledgments

This book would never have been published without the constant emotional and personal support of my boyfriend, Daniele. He lived through the second part of this story with me, the "post-mortem." He never met my mother: one day in January 2022, we went to her place to bring her masks and Covid tests we had just bought. Daniele stayed in the car while I went up and left the bag in front of the door. Unfortunately, my mother was in the throes of a Covid-19 infection, and I couldn't meet her in person. It was heartbreaking to say goodbye through the window; that was the only moment my boyfriend and my mother "met" and greeted each other with a wave.

Daniele accompanied me that day to the hospital, where we saw my mother's lifeless body. He saw all our pain when we left because our mother was no longer there. He held my hand at the funeral, and if it hadn't been for him supporting me, I don't know how I would have endured that indescribable pain. Daniele cried with me, got angry with me, because my mother didn't deserve this: no one deserves such treatment.

Daniele has been by my side through every moment of this ordeal, from meetings with lawyers to those at the bank, even that day when we were sitting at the table with the notary and HIM, who was sitting across from him. He later confided in me that he noticed a certain embarrassment in HIM, which pleased me particularly; he also noticed that HE often sought my gaze, but seeing that I denied it to him, he swore he saw profound sadness in HIM.

Daniele was, like me, a witness to this profound injustice and always pushed me not to give up, even though everyone around me said this was a lost battle.

I thank my family, especially my uncles. My uncle Libero, my mother's brother, accompanied me physically and psychologically through this tough succession process. Without him, I don't think I would have been able to withstand all these abuses.

I wholeheartedly thank my mother's friends and colleagues, who showed affection, understanding, and support to my sister and me from the very first moment. Even though we had never met many of them, it was as if they knew us. My mother constantly talked about us and made sure to share our achievements and successes, telling everyone how proud she was of her daughters.

I thank the people who showed me affection and support, backing and sharing my petition. I thank everyone who took an interest in my case, the journalists, and the newsrooms, who tried to shed light on a situation that POLITICS should have remedied.

I thank the people I met during my work as an educator, who always listened and supported me, especially the children, girls, and boys. I hope they have fond memories of me and that my advice and "teachings" were a light for them in moments of pain and discomfort.

I thank my university colleagues who showed affection and supported my battle, as well as some professors who showed humanity in understanding my difficulties following this event. I managed to graduate on October 15, 2023, which is one of the achievements I never thought I would reach in my life. I would have loved for my mother to be there: it is also thanks to her that I could continue my studies, because she helped and always supported me in pursuing this path.

I thank my mother for giving me the strength necessary to endure all the pain and fight against what we consider profound injustices. My mother always said that there was a solution to everything. Every time I had a problem, she would say, "we need to come up with a plan."

I hope someone devises a plan for her and all the people like her who have been victims of violence. I hope that someone will stop handing over my "father" the pension, the fruit of so many sacrifices and my mother's work. I hope that someone notices the severe legislative gap that allows this injustice; I hope the legislators' will has changed.

Unfortunately, I have tried everything; my plan, Mom, has failed. This is my last desperate cry.

Thank you to those who will listen.

Printed in Great Britain
by Amazon